Transcribe by ANDY ROBYNS

NIRVANA
INCESTICIDE

ISBN 0-7935-2761-9

7777 W. BLUEMOUND RD. P.O. BOX 13819 MILWAUKEE, WI 53213

Copyright © 1995 by HAL LEONARD CORPORATION
International Copyright Secured   All Rights Reserved

For all works contained herein:
Unauthorized copying, arranging, adapting, recording or public performance is an infringement of copyright.
Infringers are liable under the law.

Photo by Charles Peterson

NIRVANA
INCESTICIDE

66 ANEURYSM
21 BEEN A SON
37 BEESWAX
62 BIG LONG NOW
 9 DIVE
41 DOWNER
49 HAIRSPRAY QUEEN
45 MEXICAN SEAFOOD
29 MOLLY'S LIPS
34 (NEW WAVE) POLLY
13 SLIVER
31 SON OF A GUN
16 STAIN
24 TURNAROUND
71 NOTATION LEGEND

Photo by Charles Peterson

Photo by Charles Peterson

Photo by Charles Peterson

Photo by Charles Peterson

Photo by Charles Peterson

Dive

By Kurt Cobain and Chris Novoselic

* Play natural harmonic on the 5th string 4/10 then 9/10 the distance between the 2nd and 3rd frets.

© 1989 EMI VIRGIN SONGS, INC. and THE END OF MUSIC
All Rights Controlled and Administered by EMI VIRGIN SONGS, INC. (BMI)
All Rights Reserved   International Copyright Secured   Used By Permission

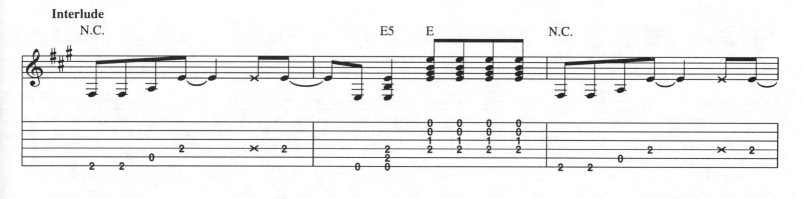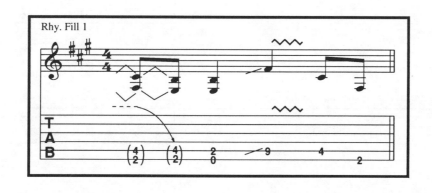

11

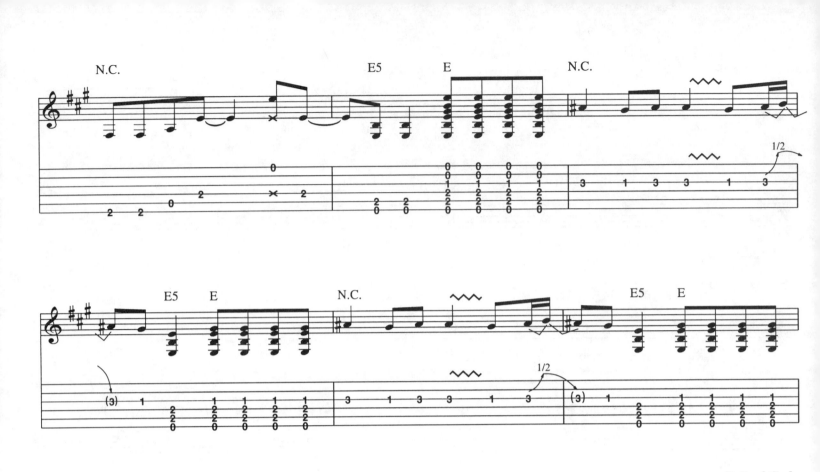
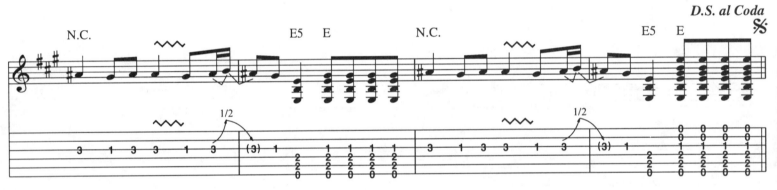

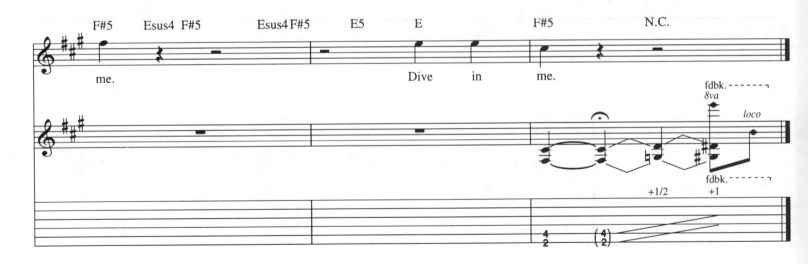

Sliver

By Kurt Cobain

© 1989 EMI Virgin Songs, INC. and THE END OF MUSIC
All Rights Controlled and Administered by EMI VIRGIN SONGS, INC. (BMI)
All Rights Reserved   International Copyright Secured   Used By Permission

13

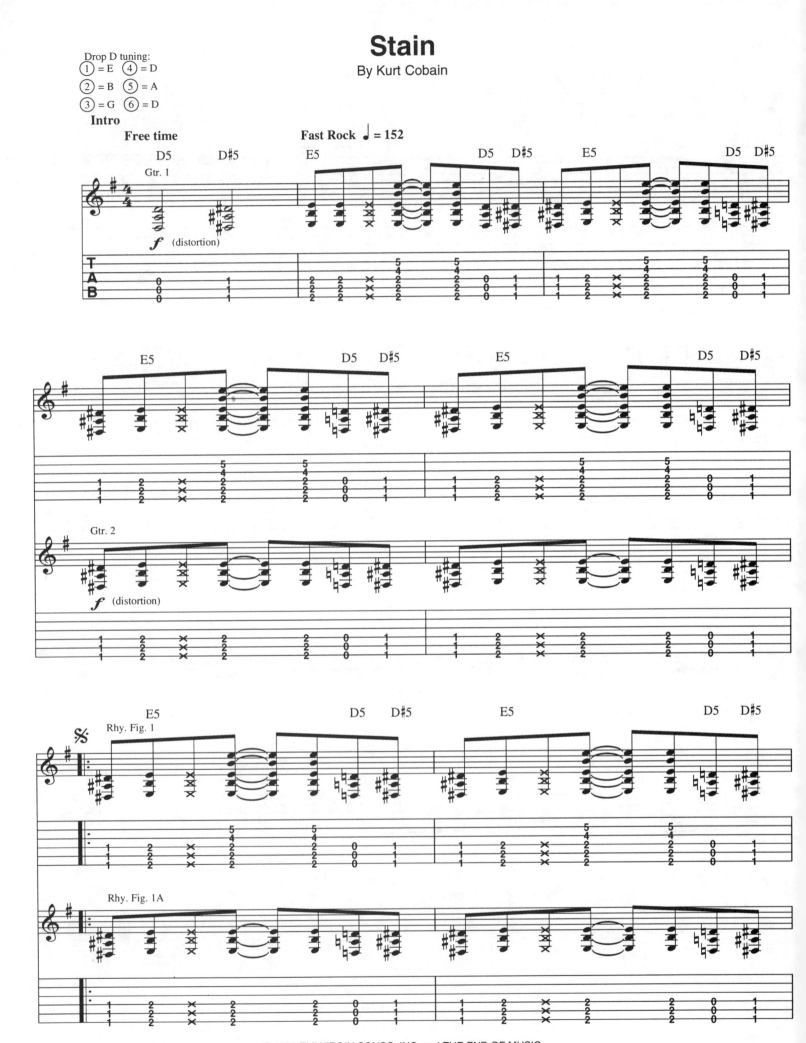

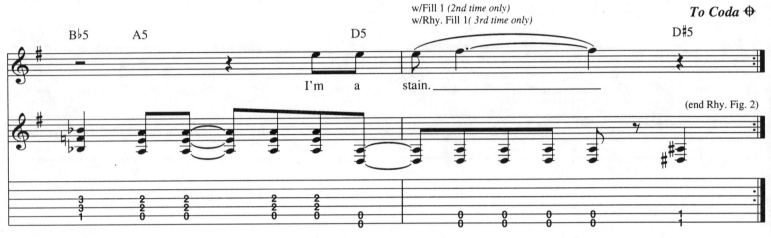
Guitar Solo
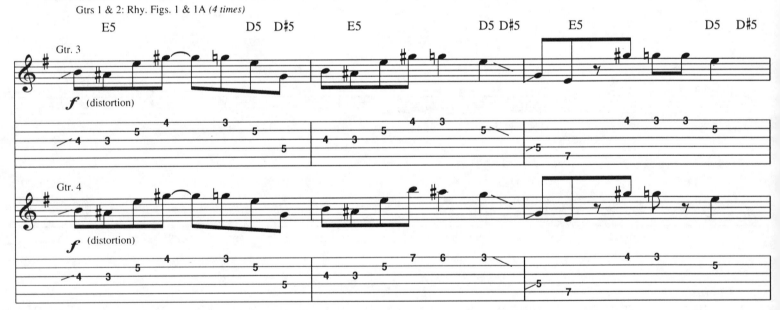
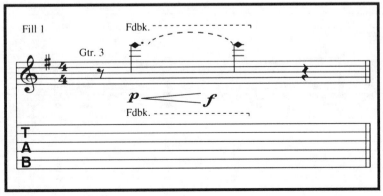
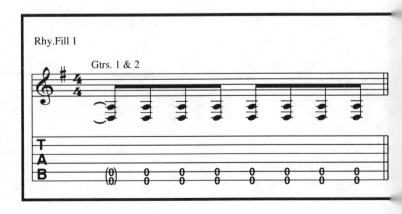

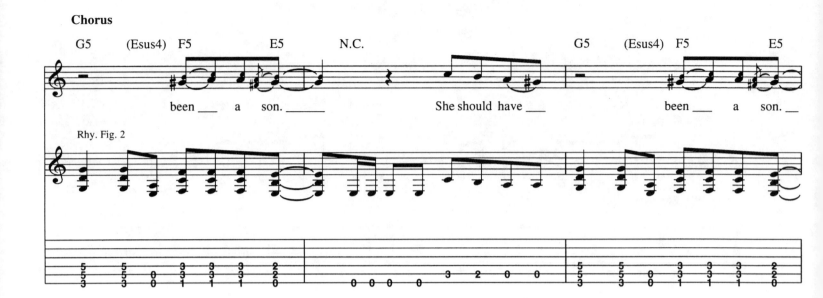
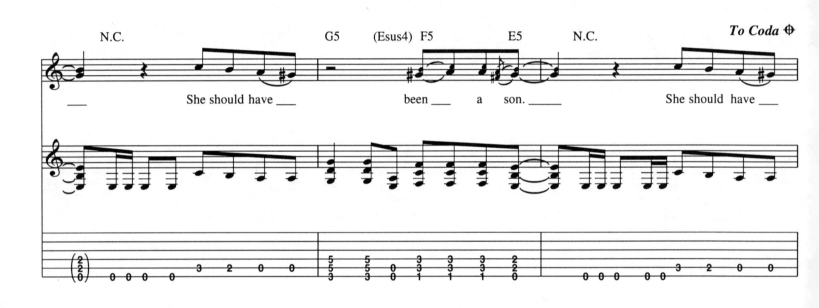
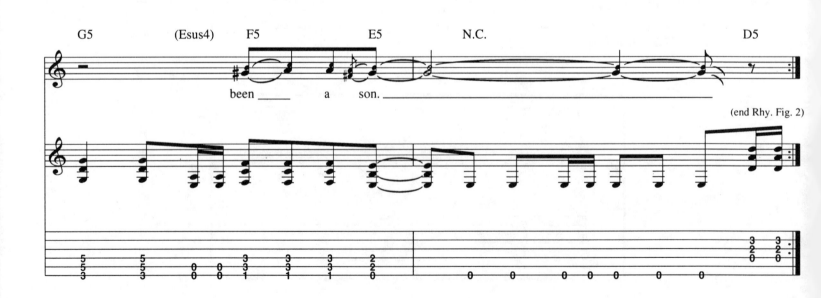

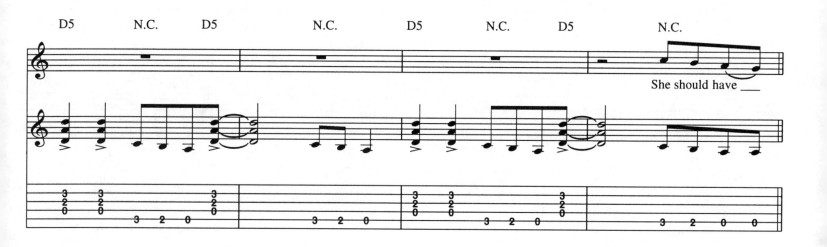

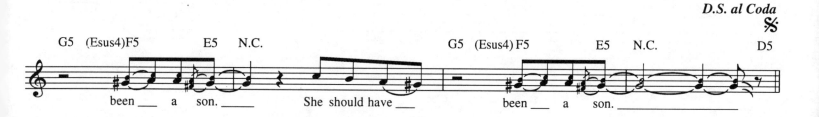
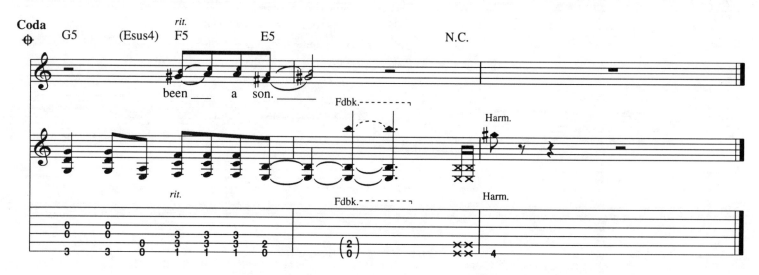

Turnaround

By Mark Mothersbaugh and Gerald Casale

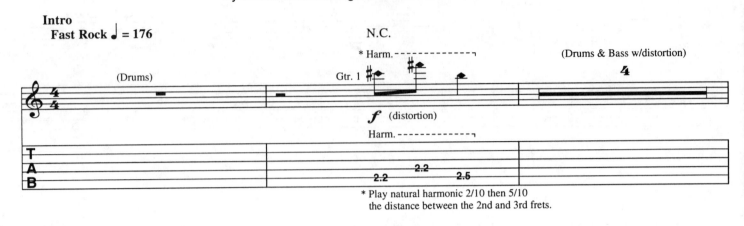

*Play natural harmonic 2/10 then 5/10 the distance between the 2nd and 3rd frets.

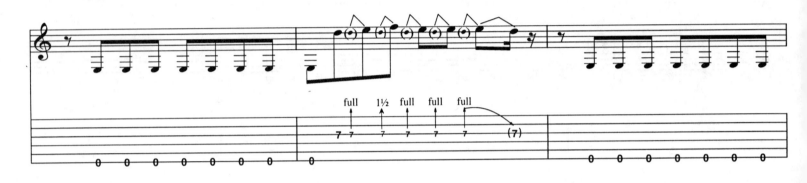

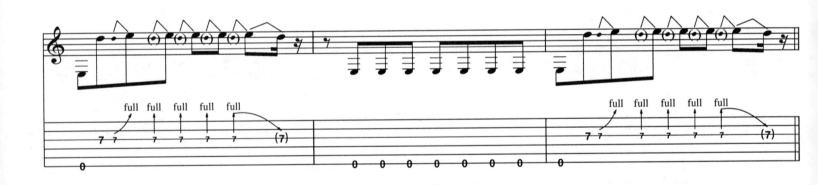

Take a step out of your-self,
Take a step out-side the cit - y,
Take a step out of the coun - try,

© 1980 EMI VIRGIN MUSIC LTD.
All Rights for the U.S.A. and Canada Controlled and Administered by EMI VIRGIN SONGS, INC. (BMI)
All Rights Reserved International Copyright Secured Used By Permission

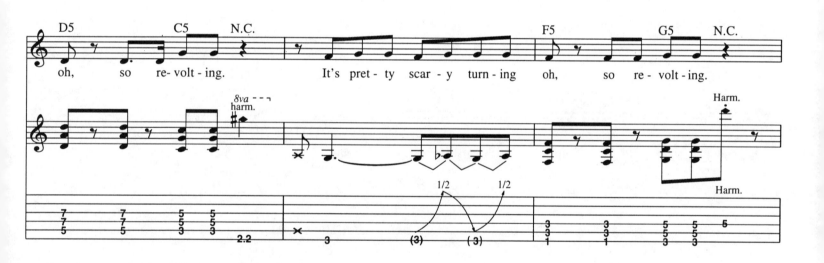

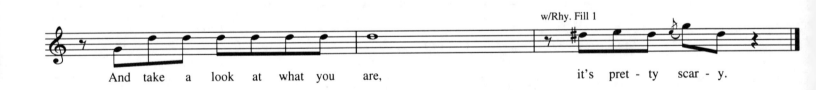

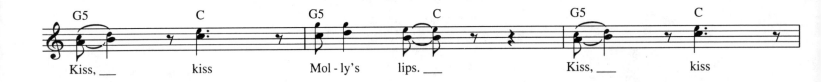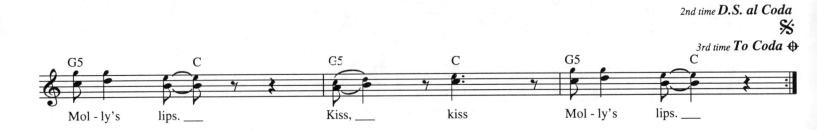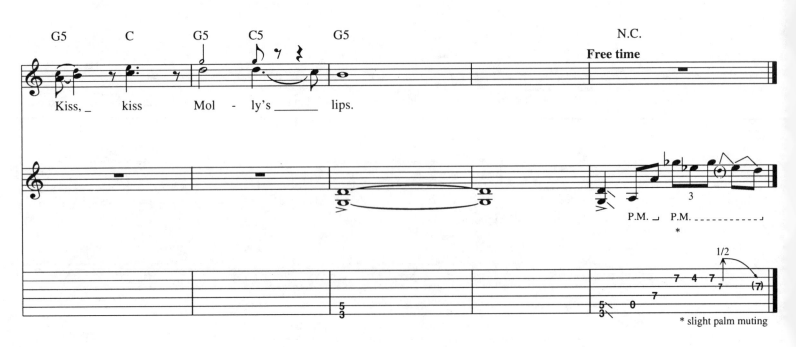

Son Of A Gun

Words and Music by
Frances McKee and Eugene Kelly

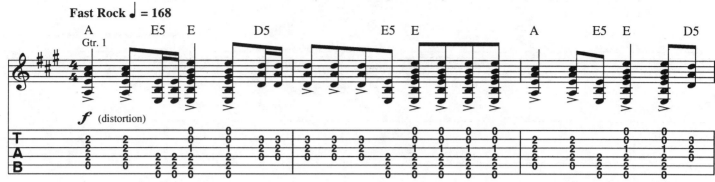
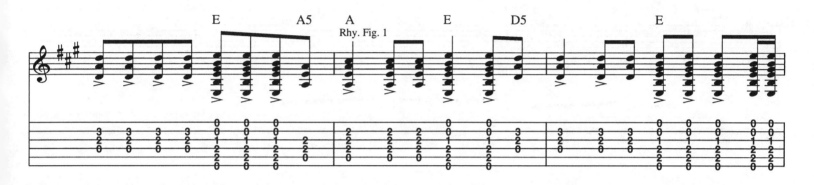
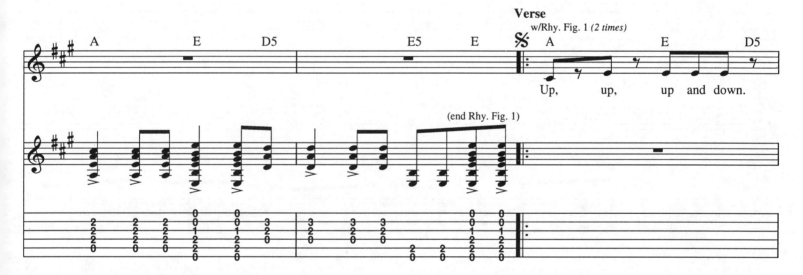
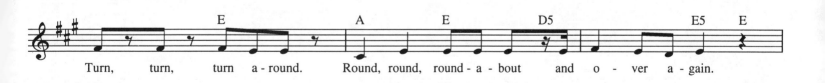

Turn, turn, turn a-round. Round, round, round-a-bout and o-ver a-gain.

Gun, gun, son of a gun, you are the on-ly one that makes an-y dif-ference in

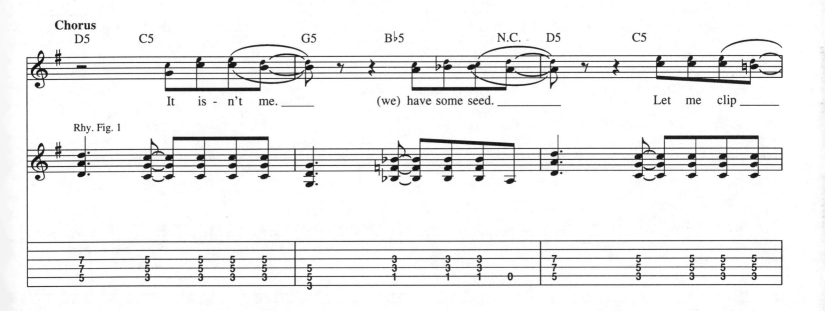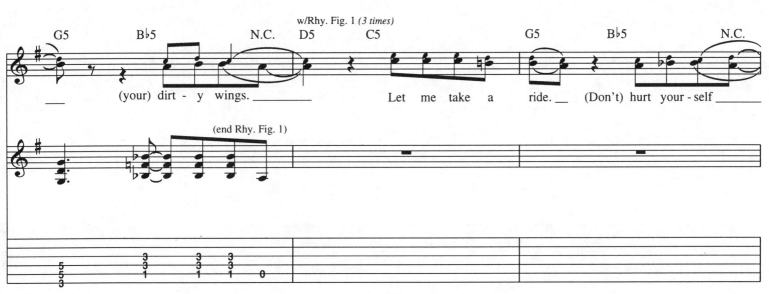

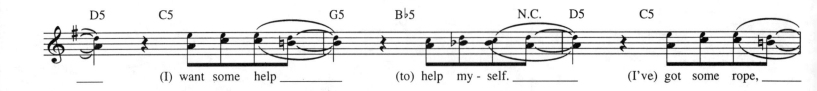
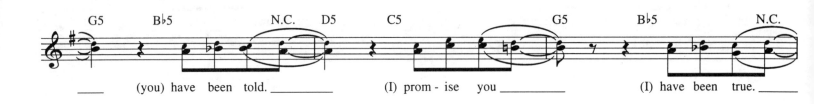
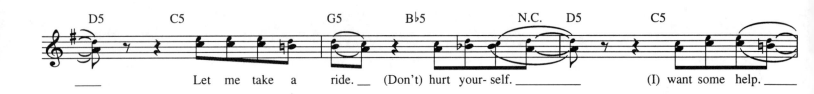
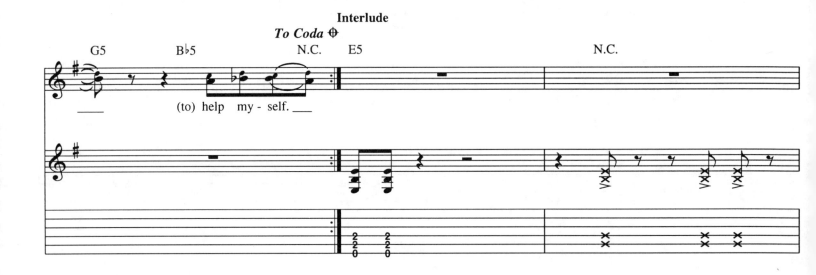
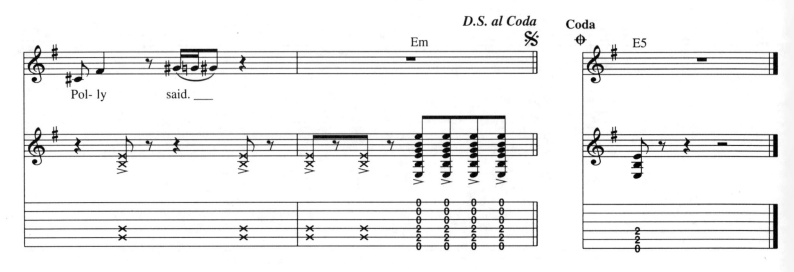

39

Downer
by Kurt Cobain

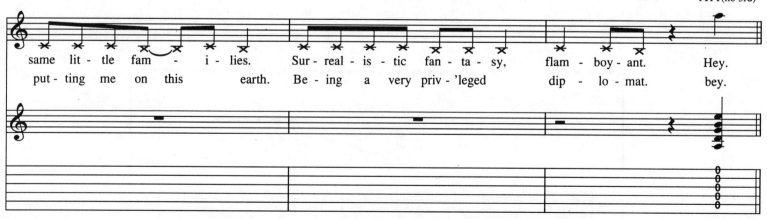

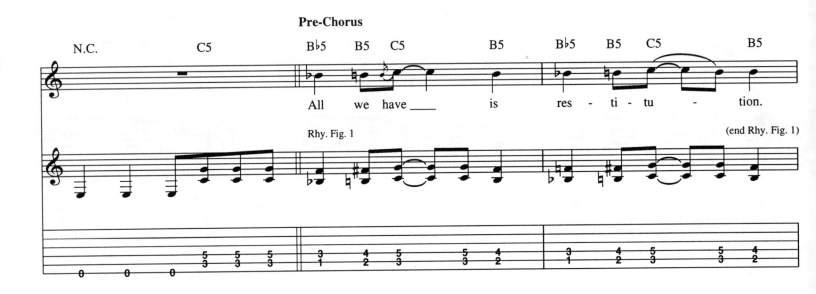

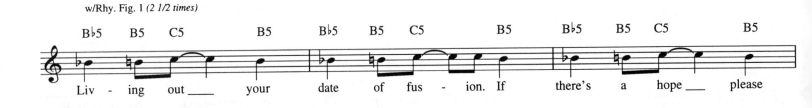

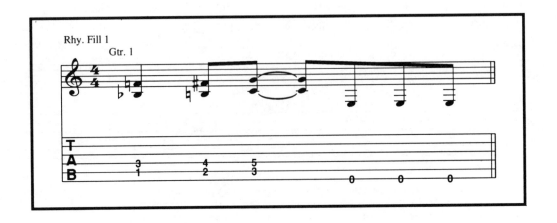

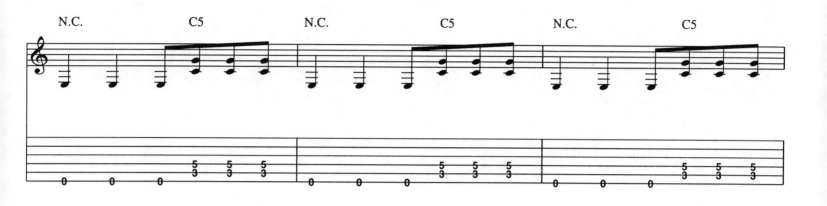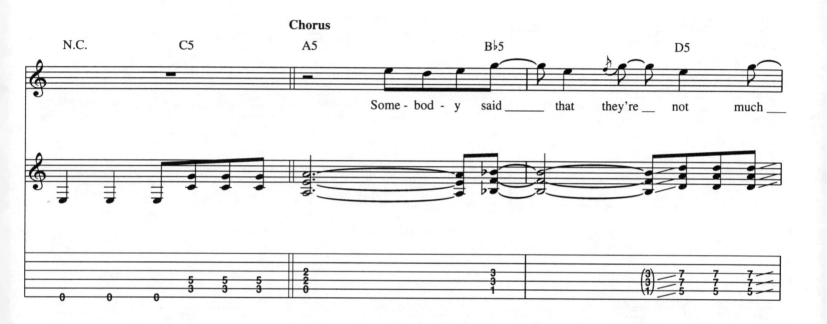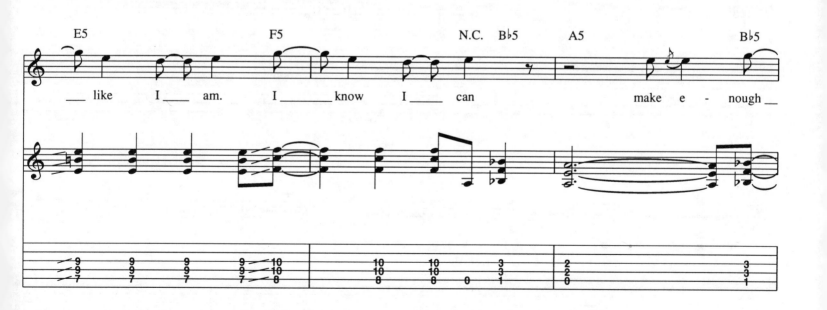

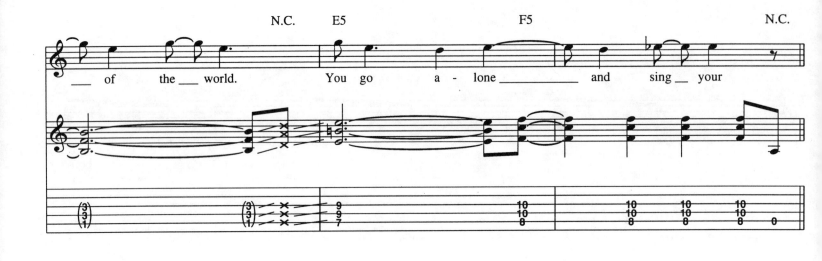

Outro

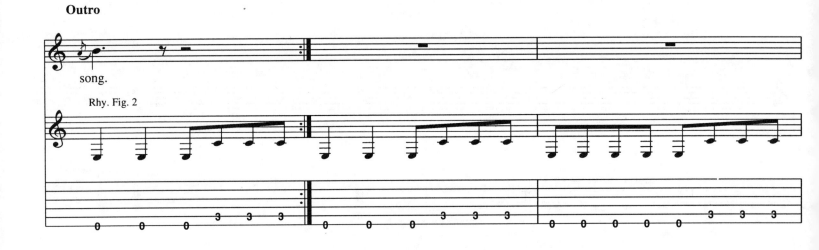

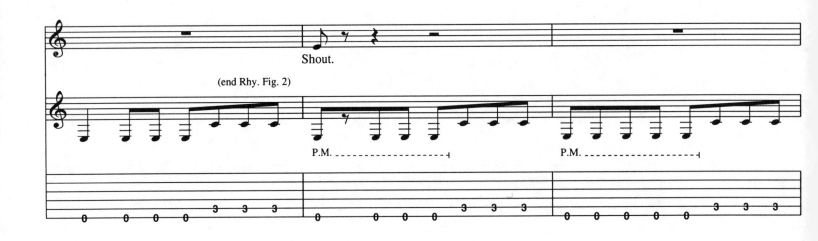

Mexican Seafood

By Kurt Cobain

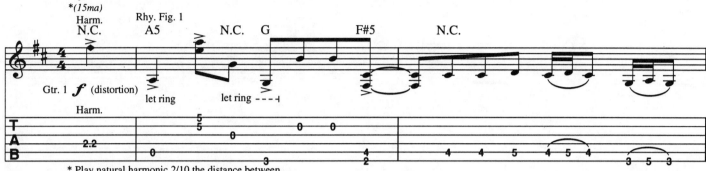

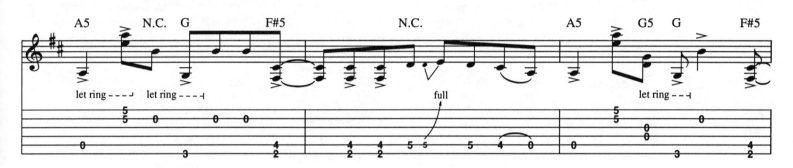

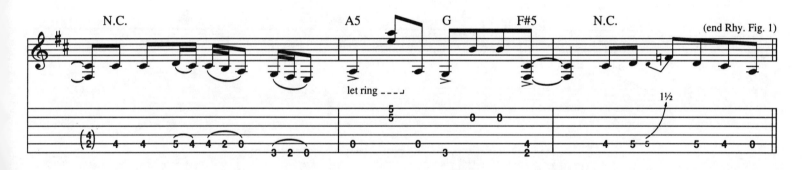

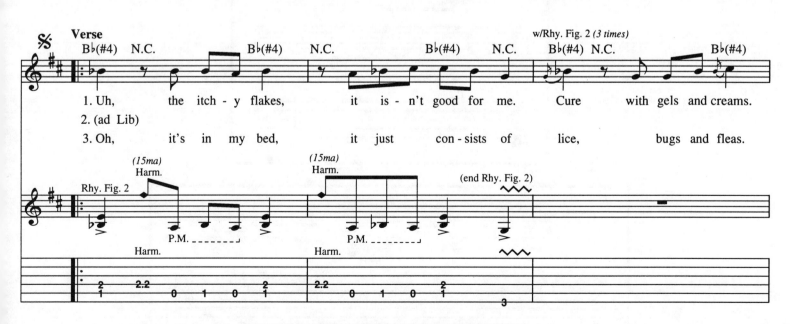

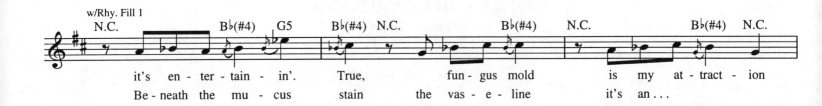

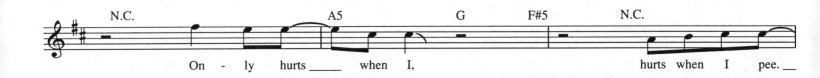

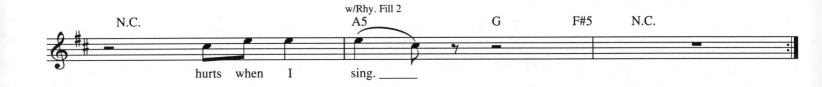

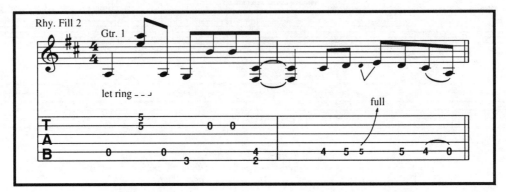

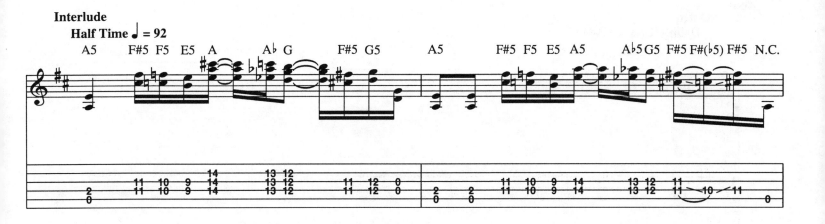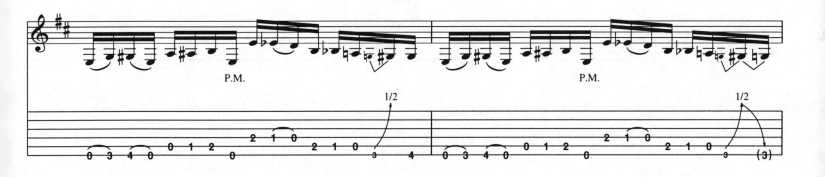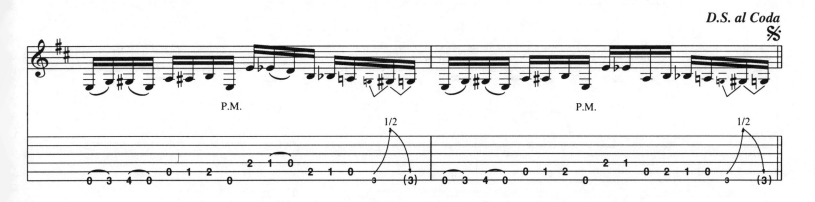

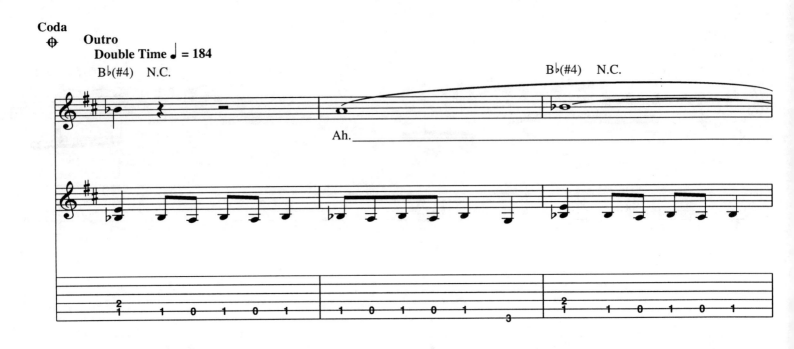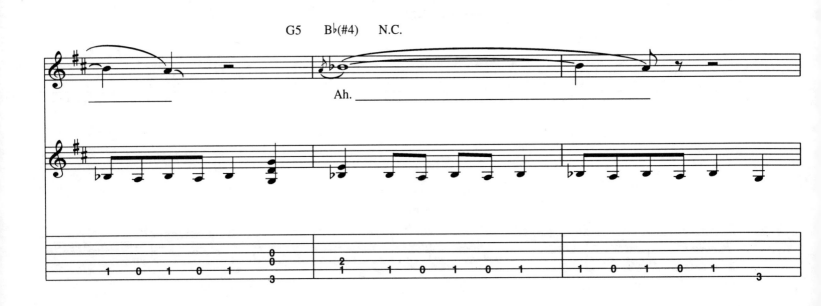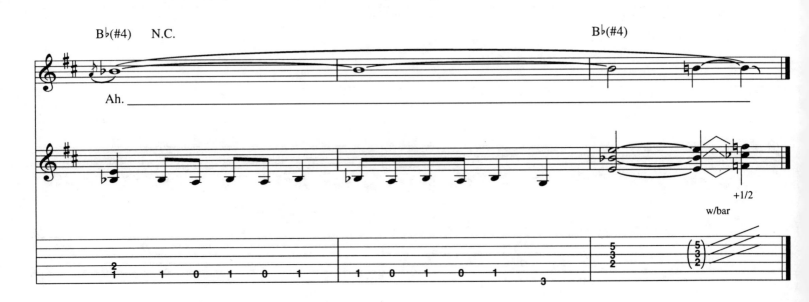

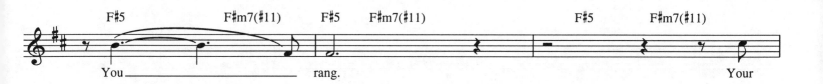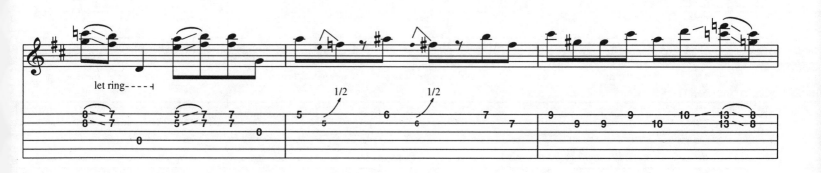

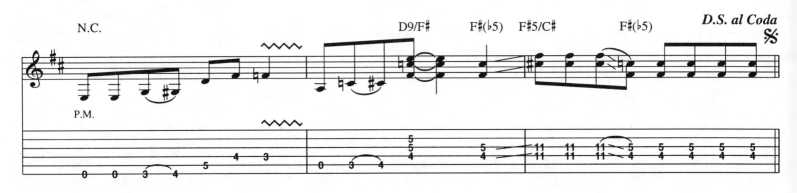

Coda
Chorus
w/Rhy. Fig. 3

At night the crystal locket. At night, a mouth full of almonds.

At sight a fish full of garbage. At night the disco god.

4th Guitar Solo
(Ad-lib Vocal screams next 8 measures)

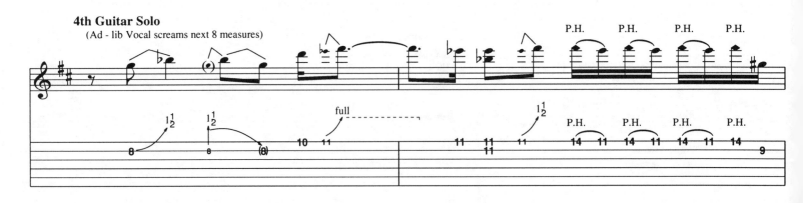
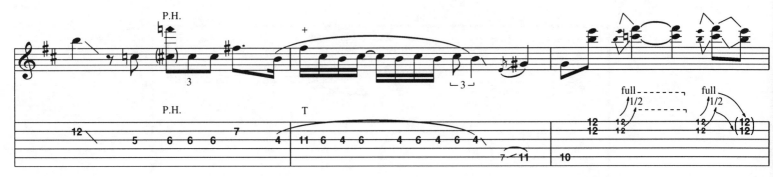

Outro

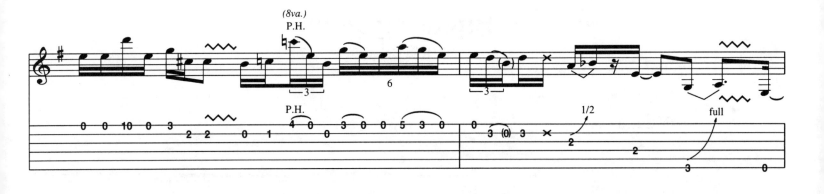

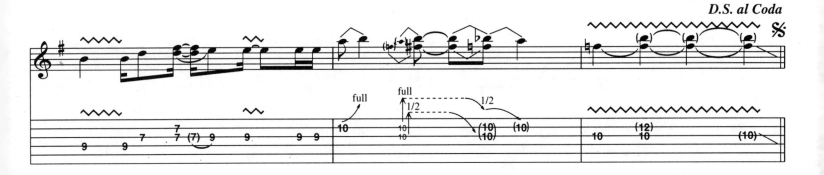

Coda
Outro

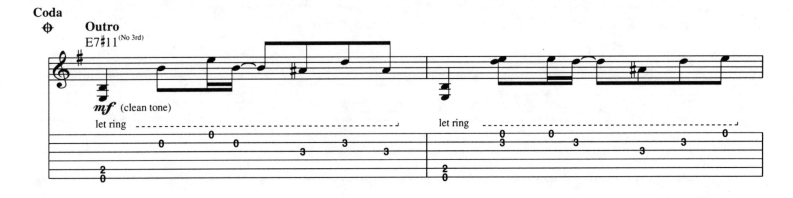
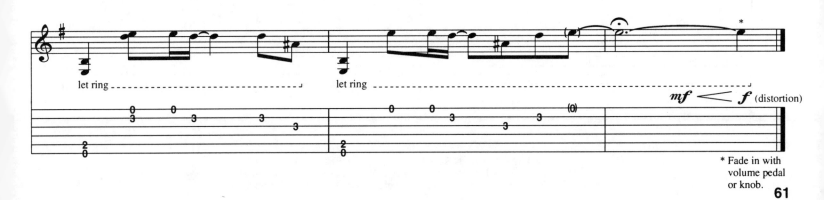

*Fade in with volume pedal or knob.

Big Long Now

By Kurt Cobain

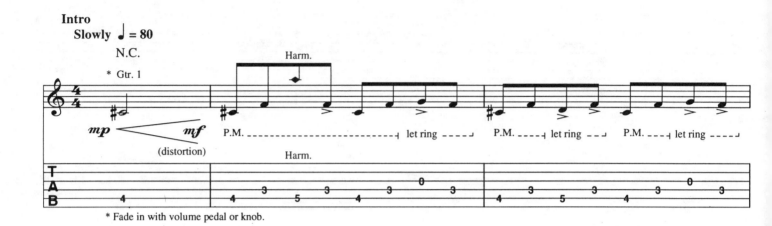

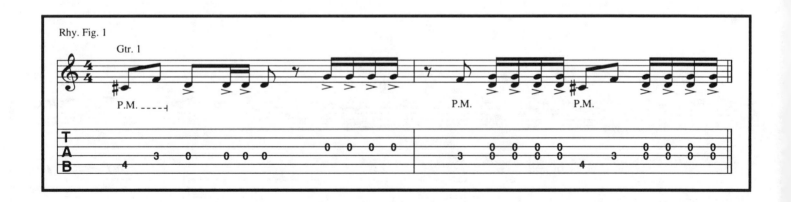

© 1989 EMI VIRGIN SONGS, INC. and THE END OF MUSIC
All Rights Controlled and Administered by EMI VIRGIN SONGS, INC. (BMI)
All Rights Reserved   International Copyright Secured   Used By Permission

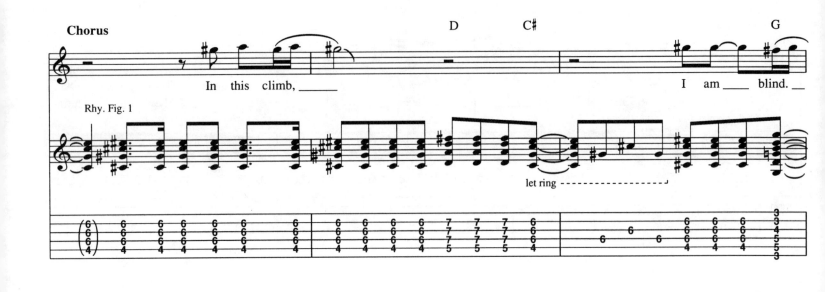
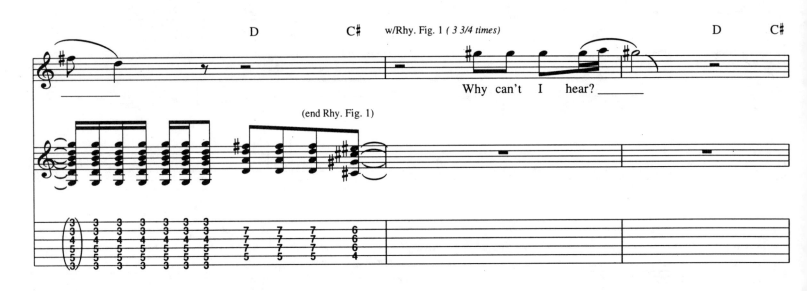

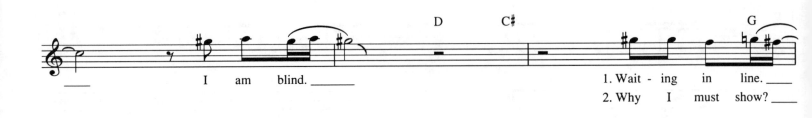

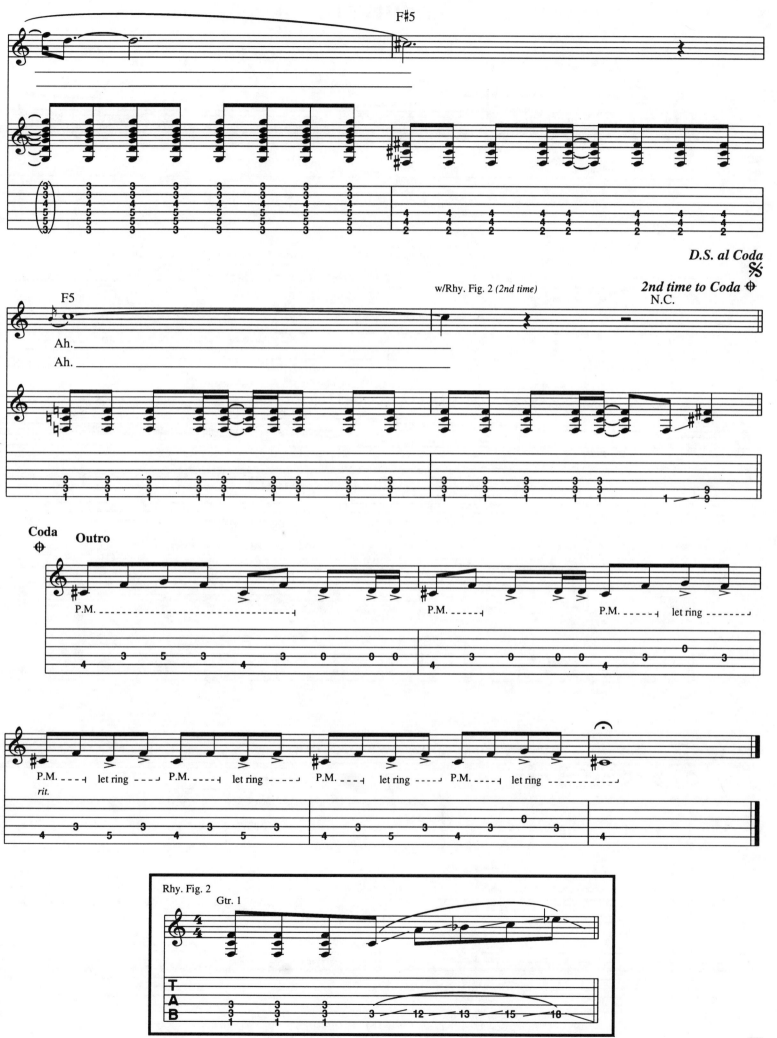

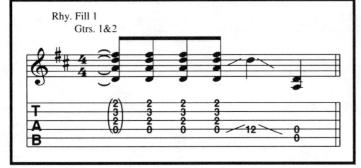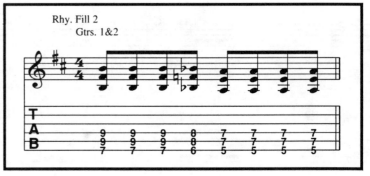

NOTATION LEGEND

RECORDED VERSIONS
The Best Note-For-Note Transcriptions Available

ALL BOOKS INCLUDE TABLATURE

00690002	Aerosmith – Big Ones	$22.95
00694909	Aerosmith – Get A Grip	$19.95
00692015	Aerosmith's Greatest Hits	$19.95
00660133	Aerosmith – Pump	$19.95
00694865	Alice In Chains – Dirt	$19.95
00660225	Alice In Chains – Facelift	$19.95
00694925	Alice In Chains – Jar Of Flies/Sap	$19.95
00694932	Allman Brothers Band – Vol. 1	$24.95
00694933	Allman Brothers Band – Vol. 2	$24.95
00694934	Allman Brothers Band – Vol. 3	$24.95
00694826	Anthrax – Attack Of The Killer B's	$19.95
00694876	Chet Atkins – Contemporary Styles	$19.95
00694918	The Randy Bachman Collection	$22.95
00660051	Badlands	$19.95
00694929	Beatles: 1962-1966	$24.95
00694930	Beatles: 1967-1970	$24.95
00694880	Beatles – Abbey Road	$19.95
00694832	Beatles For Acoustic Guitar	$19.95
00660140	Beatles Guitar Book	$19.95
00694891	Beatles – Revolver	$19.95
00694914	Beatles – Rubber Soul	$19.95
00694863	Beatles – Sgt. Pepper's Lonely Hearts Club Band	$19.95
00694931	Belly – Star	$19.95
00694884	The Best of George Benson	$19.95
00692385	Chuck Berry	$19.95
00692200	Black Sabbath – We Sold Our Soul For Rock 'N' Roll	$19.95
00694821	Blue Heaven – Great Blues Guitar	$19.95
00694770	Jon Bon Jovi – Blaze Of Glory	$19.95
00690008	Bon Jovi – Cross Road	$19.95
00694871	Bon Jovi – Keep The Faith	$19.95
00694775	Bon Jovi – Slippery When Wet	$19.95
00694935	Boston: Double Shot Of Boston	$22.95
00694762	Cinderella – Heartbreak Station	$19.95
00692376	Cinderella – Long Cold Winter	$19.95
00692375	Cinderella – Night Songs	$19.95
00694875	Eric Clapton – Boxed Set	$75.00
00692392	Eric Clapton – Crossroads Vol. 1	$22.95
00692393	Eric Clapton – Crossroads Vol. 2	$22.95
00692394	Eric Clapton – Crossroads Vol. 3	$22.95
00690010	Eric Clapton – From The Cradle	$19.95
00660139	Eric Clapton – Journeyman	$19.95
00694869	Eric Clapton – Unplugged	$19.95
00692391	The Best of Eric Clapton	$19.95
00694896	John Mayall/Eric Clapton – Bluesbreakers	$19.95
00694873	Eric Clapton – Timepieces	$19.95
00694837	Albert Collins – The Complete Imperial Recordings	$19.95
00694862	Contemporary Country Guitar	$18.95
00660127	Alice Cooper – Trash	$19.95
00694941	Crash Test Dummies – God Shuffled His Feet	$19.95
00694840	Cream – Disraeli Gears	$19.95
00690033	Danzig – Prime Cuts	$19.95
00690007	Danzig 4	$19.95
00690034	Danzig	$18.95
00694844	Def Leppard – Adrenalize	$19.95
00660186	Alex De Grassi Guitar Collection	$19.95
00694831	Derek And The Dominos – Layla & Other Assorted Love Songs	$19.95
00692240	Bo Diddley Guitar Solos	$19.95
00660175	Dio – Lock Up The Wolves	$19.95
00660178	Willie Dixon	$24.95
00694915	Electric Blues Guitar Giants	$18.95
00694800	FireHouse	$18.95
00694867	FireHouse – Hold Your Fire	$19.95
00694920	Best of Free	$18.95
00694894	Frank Gambale – The Great Explorers	$19.95
00694807	Danny Gatton – 88 Elmira St	$19.95
00694848	Genuine Rockabilly Guitar Hits	$19.95
00694798	George Harrison Anthology	$19.95
00690068	Return of The Hellecasters	$19.95
00692930	Jimi Hendrix – Are You Experienced?	$19.95
00692931	Jimi Hendrix – Axis: Bold As Love	$19.95
00694944	Jimi Hendrix – Blues	$24.95
00660192	The Jimi Hendrix – Concerts	$24.95
00692932	Jimi Hendrix – Electric Ladyland	$24.95
00694923	Jimi Hendrix – The Experience Collection Boxed Set	$75.00
00660099	Jimi Hendrix – Radio One	$24.95
00694919	Jimi Hendrix – Stone Free	$19.95
00660024	Jimi Hendrix – Variations On A Theme: Red House	$19.95
00660029	Buddy Holly	$19.95
00660200	John Lee Hooker – The Healer	$19.95
00660169	John Lee Hooker – A Blues Legend	$19.95
00694850	Iron Maiden – Fear Of The Dark	$19.95
00694938	Elmore James – Master Electric Slide Guitar	$14.95
00694833	Billy Joel For Guitar	$19.95
00660147	Eric Johnson	$19.95
00694912	Eric Johnson – Ah Via Musicom	$19.95
00694911	Eric Johnson – Tones	$19.95
00694799	Robert Johnson – At The Crossroads	$19.95
00693186	Judas Priest – Metal Cuts	$19.95
00660226	Judas Priest – Painkiller	$19.95
00693187	Judas Priest – Ram It Down	$19.95
00693185	Judas Priest – Vintage Hits	$19.95
00694764	Kentucky Headhunters – Pickin' On Nashville	$19.95
00694795	Kentucky Headhunters – Electric Barnyard	$19.95
00660050	B. B. King	$19.95
00694903	The Best Of Kiss	$24.95
00694806	L.A. Guns – Hollywood Vampires	$18.95
00694794	Best Of Los Lobos	$18.95
00660199	The Lynch Mob – Wicked Sensation	$19.95
00694954	Lynyrd Skynyrd, New Best Of	$19.95
00660174	Yngwie Malmsteen – Eclipse	$19.95
00694845	Yngwie Malmsteen – Fire And Ice	$19.95
00694750	Yngwie Malmsteen – Marching Out	$19.95
00694755	Yngwie Malmsteen – Rising Force	$19.95
00660001	Yngwie Malmsteen's Rising Force – Odyssey	$19.95
00694757	Yngwie Malmsteen – Trilogy	$19.95
00694956	Bob Marley – Legend	$19.95
00690020	Meat Loaf – Bat Out Of Hell I & II	$22.95
00694952	Megadeth – Countdown To Extinction	$19.95
00694951	Megadeth – Rust In Peace	$22.95
00694953	Megadeth – Selections From "Peace Sells...But Who's Buying?" & "So Far, So Good...So What!"	$22.95
00692880	Metal Madness	$17.95
00694792	Metal Church – The Human Factor	$19.95
00694868	Gary Moore – After Hours	$19.95
00694849	Gary Moore – The Early Years	$19.95
00694802	Gary Moore – Still Got The Blues	$19.95
00694872	Vinnie Moore – Meltdown	$19.95
00694958	Mountain, Best Of	$19.95
00694895	Nirvana – Bleach	$19.95
00694913	Nirvana – In Utero	$19.95
00694883	Nirvana – Nevermind	$19.95
00690026	Nirvana – Unplugged In New York	$19.95
00694847	Best Of Ozzy Osbourne	$22.95
00694830	Ozzy Osbourne – No More Tears	$19.95
00694855	Pearl Jam – Ten	$19.95
00693800	Pink Floyd – Early Classics	$19.95
00693864	Police, The Best Of	$18.95
00692535	Elvis Presley	$18.95
00694975	Queen – Classic	$24.95
00694974	Queen – A Night At The Opera	$19.95
00694969	Queensryche – Selections from "Operation: Mindcrime"	$19.95
00694910	Rage Against The Machine	$19.95
00693910	Ratt – Invasion of Your Privacy	$19.95
00693911	Ratt – Out Of The Cellar	$19.95
00690027	Red Hot Chili Peppers – Out In L.A.	$19.95
00694968	Red Hot Chili Peppers – Selections from "What Hits!?"	$22.95
00694892	Guitar Style Of Jerry Reed	$19.95
00694899	REM – Automatic For The People	$19.95
00694898	REM – Out Of Time	$19.95
00660060	Robbie Robertson	$19.95
00694959	Rockin' Country Guitar	$19.95
00690014	Rolling Stones – Exile On Main Street	$24.95
00694976	Rolling Stones – Some Girls	$18.95
00694897	Roots Of Country Guitar	$19.95
00694836	Richie Sambora – Stranger In This Town	$19.95
00694805	Scorpions – Crazy World	$19.95
00694916	Scorpions – Face The Heat	$19.95
00694870	Seattle Scene	$18.95
00694885	Spin Doctors – Pocket Full Of Kryptonite	$19.95
00694962	Spin Doctors – Turn It Upside Down	$19.95
00694917	Spin Doctors – Up For Grabs	$19.95
00694796	Steelheart	$19.95
00694921	Steppenwolf, The Best Of	$22.95
00694801	Rod Stewart, Best Of	$22.95
00694957	Rod Stewart – Unplugged...And Seated	$22.95
00694180	Stryper – In God We Trust	$19.95
00694824	Best Of James Taylor	$16.95
00694846	Testament – The Ritual	$19.95
00694887	Thin Lizzy – The Best Of Thin Lizzy	$19.95
00694410	The Best of U2	$19.95
00694411	U2 – The Joshua Tree	$19.95
00660137	Steve Vai – Passion & Warfare	$24.95
00694904	Vai – Sex and Religion	$24.95
00694879	Stevie Ray Vaughan – In The Beginning	$19.95
00660136	Stevie Ray Vaughan – In Step	$19.95
00660058	Stevie Ray Vaughan – Lightnin' Blues 1983 – 1987	$24.95
00694835	Stevie Ray Vaughan – The Sky Is Crying	$19.95
00690015	Stevie Ray Vaughan – Texas Flood	$19.95
00690024	Stevie Ray Vaughan – Couldn't Stand The Weather	$19.95
00694776	Vaughan Brothers – Family Style	$19.95
00660196	Vixen – Rev It Up	$19.95
00694781	Warrant – Cherry Pie	$19.95
00694787	Warrant – Dirty Rotten Filthy Stinking Rich	$19.95
00694866	Warrant – Dog Eat Dog	$19.95
00694789	The Muddy Waters Guitar Collection	$24.95
00694888	Windham Hill Guitar Sampler	$18.95
00694786	Winger	$19.95
00694782	Winger – In The Heart Of The Young	$19.95
00694900	Winger – Pull	$19.95

Prices and availability subject to change without notice. Some products may not be available outside the U.S.A.

FOR MORE INFORMATION, SEE YOUR LOCAL MUSIC DEALER, OR WRITE TO:

0595